Ani...

...en

Smith

Please return/renew this item by the last date shown to avoid a charge. Books may also be renewed by phone and Internet. May not be renewed if required by another reader.

www.libraries.barnet.gov.uk

BARNET
LONDON BOROUGH

Raintree is an imprint of Capstone Global Library Limited, a company incorporated in England and Wales having its registered office at 7 Pilgrim Street, London, EC4V 6LB – Registered company number: 6695582

www.raintreepublishers.co.uk
myorders@raintreepublishers.co.uk

Text © Capstone Global Library Limited 2015
First published in hardback in 2014
Paperback edition first published in 2015
The moral rights of the proprietor have been asserted.

Edited by Siân Smith, John-Paul Wilkins and Helen Cox Cannons
Designed by Cynthia Akiyoshi
Picture research by Mica Brancic and Tracy Cummins
Production by Victoria Fitzgerald
Originated by Capstone Global Library
Printed and bound in China

ISBN 978 1 406 28052 4 (hardback)
18 17 16 15 14
10 9 8 7 6 5 4 3 2 1

ISBN 978 1 406 28057 9 (paperback)
19 18 17 16 15
10 9 8 7 6 5 4 3 2 1

British Library Cataloguing in Publication Data
A full catalogue record for this book is available from the British Library.

Acknowledgements
We would like to thank the following for permission to reproduce photographs: Shutterstock pp. 1 (© ivosar), 2 (© Ultrashock), 3 left (© PhotoEd), 3 middle, 20 top right (© Pan Xunbin), 3 right (© Robert Eastman), 4 (© Vaclav Volrab), 5 (© StevenRussellSmithPhotos), 6 (© Dragoness), 7 (© Martin Fowler), 8 (© S. Cooper Digital), 9 (© Mauro Rodrigues), 10 (© Menno Schaefer), 11 (© alexsvirid), 12, 22b (© xfox01), 13, 21 (© Lorelinka), 14 (© Dani Vincek), 15 (© craigbirdphotos), 16 (© Santia), 17 (© papkin), 18, 22a (© Andrey Pavlov), 19 (© Photo Fun), 20 bottom left (© Azaliya), 20 bottom right (© Chris Howey), 20 top left (© Evgeniy Ayupov).

Front cover photograph of a mole reproduced with kind permission of Shutterstock (© mradlgruber). Back cover photographs reproduced with permission of Shutterstock (© PhotoEd, © Robert Eastman, © Pan Xunbin).

Every effort has been made to contact copyright holders of material reproduced in this book. Any omissions will be rectified in subsequent printings if notice is given to the publisher.

Contents

Garden animals

Can you see the hedgehog?

Can you see the butterfly?

Can you see the frog?

Can you see the wasp?

Can you see the squirrel?

Can you see the woodlouse?

Can you see the fox?

Can you see the worm?

Can you see the slug?

Can you see the snail?

Can you see the bee?

Can you see the bird?

Can you see the mole?

Can you see the spider?

Can you see the ant?

Can you see the ladybird?

What can you see?

Try looking under logs or stones in a garden. Can you see these animals?

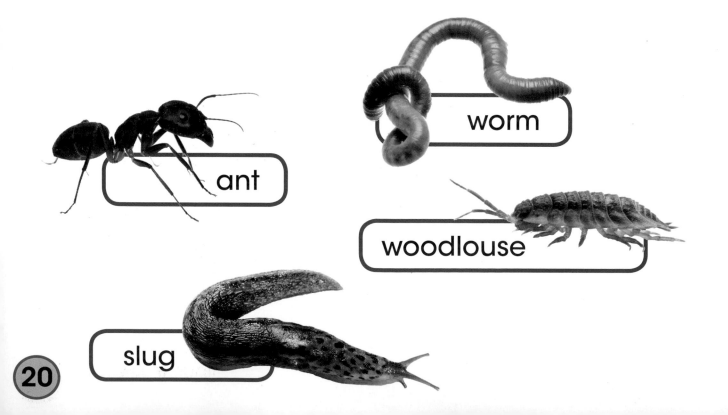

worm

ant

woodlouse

slug

What am I?

I have one foot.

I eat plants.

I leave a trail of slime.

I carry a shell on my back.

Picture glossary

 ant

 slug

Index

Notes for teachers and parents

Before reading

Tuning in: Talk about animals the child has seen in a garden or in the park. Which creature spins a web? Which creature has 7 spots?

After reading

Recall and reflection: Which animals in the garden can fly? Which animals in the garden have a tail?

Sentence knowledge: Help the child to count the number of words in each sentence.

Word knowledge (phonics): Encourage the child to point at the word 'can' on any page. Sound out the phonemes in the word 'c/a/n'. Ask the child to sound out each letter as they point at it and then blend the sounds together to make the word 'can'.

Word recognition: Challenge the child to race you to point at the word 'you' on any page.

Rounding off

Play a syllable clapping game: say the names of some of the animals. Ask the child to clap the number of syllables in the word, e.g. ladybird (3) spider (2) butterfly (3) hedgehog (2).

Word coverage

Sentence stem

Can you see the _____?

High-frequency words

can
see
the
you

Ask children to read these words:

bee	p14
ant	p18
frog	p6
spider	p17

Topic words

ant
bee
bird
butterfly
fox
frog
hedgehog
ladybird
mole
slug
snail
spider
squirrel
wasp
woodlouse
worm